D1412612

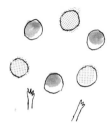

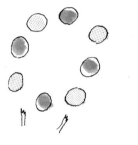

THE JUGGLER OF OUR LADY

A MEDIEVAL LEGEND
adapted by
R. O. BLECHMAN

PREFACE

∙ ∙
∙

Maurice Sendak

Published in 1997 and distributed by Stewart, Tabori & Chang,
a division of U.S. Media Holdings, Inc.
115 West 18th Street, New York, NY 10011

Distributed in Canada by General Publishing Company Ltd.
30 Lesmill Road, Don Mills, Ontario, M3B 2T6, Canada

Distributed in Australia by Peribo Pty Ltd.
58 Beaumont Road, Mount Kuring-gai, NSW 2080, Australia

Distributed in all other territories by Grantham Book Services Ltd.
Isaac Newton Way, Alma Park Industrial Estate,
Grantham, Lincolnshire, NG31 9SD, England

Library of Congress Cataloging-in-Publication Data
Blechman, R. O. (Robert O.), 1930–
The Juggler of Our Lady : a medieval legend / adapted by R.O. Blechman.
p. cm.
Originally published : New York : Holt, c1953. With a preface by Maurice Sendak
ISBN 1-55670-609-X
1. Tombeor Nostre Dame—Caricatures and cartoons. 2. American wit and humor,
Pictorial. I. Tombeor Nostre Dame. II. Title.
NC1429.B62A4 1997
741.5'973—dc21   97-3144

Printed in the United States

10 9 8 7 6 5 4 3 2 1

I WAS INTRODUCED TO R.O. BLECHMAN IN 1952, in the then-center of my universe, the Eighth Street Bookshop in Greenwich Village. It was not the flesh-and-blood Blechman—I had little hope then of knowing the man—but his spirit, voice, and immensely rich talent all manifest in a slender volume called *The Juggler of Our Lady.* It was a fine moment. I was twenty-four years old, just recently escaped from that dread *Shtetl* called Brooklyn and nursing a new career in a now-vanished, inexpensive Big Apple.

I treasure my first edition *Juggler,* and the memory of its effect on me is still fresh. I assumed, of course, that this Blechman was a wise and ancient sage; the book was rich in graphic and psychological detail, and I was busy looking for creative gurus. I've never quite recovered from the fact that Bob is younger than I am (he was born in 1930). The silliness of this detail can best be explained, perhaps, by my own 1952 consciousness of immaturity and the genuine need for a teacher outside the schoolroom.

The Juggler, delicate and modest though it was, powerfully pulled together in a single work a variety of disparate elements, which, up to that point in my career, I had imagined unjoinable. I have a very selective memory—in short, almost no memory at all, except for what passionately and selfishly serves my creative purpose. But, though *The Juggler* lies here at hand for me to refer to, I can remember that Eighth Street Bookshop Day, a day in ancient history when one could stand and read an entire book in a bookstore without surly gibes from the salesclerks. Perhaps it's wrong to linger so long over Blechman's *Juggler;* after all, it was only the beginning of a complex body of work that, astoundingly, grew constantly more subtle and refined without ever losing its secure hold on real feeling and, even more critical, its child's vision. Yet *The Juggler* is surely the ground plan for everything that came after. Simply, Blechman was Blechman in 1952 . . . *The Juggler,* in a real sense, pretty much said it all. It may be a commonplace, but there is no underestimating the pleasure to be derived from staring back over a long career and sympathetically eyeing the first work that fumblingly —even hastily—set out all the themes of one's lifetime, as if for a sumptuous but too ample dinner. My own first "grand plan" book was unabashedly if endearingly fumbling, but Blechman's was not. Now that I know Bob, I have no doubt that the entire book was tirelessly done over and over until, finally, it squeaked past the artist's harsh approval.

Only a week ago, when I visited Bob's studio for the purpose of collecting a mass of Blechmaniana for this introduction, I asked him for a copy of *The Juggler* to peruse. (I did not want to flip through my personal copy, and Bob is a sufficient book nut to understand such finickiness.) He promptly presented me with a first edition—autographed to Ronald Searle. I was a little taken aback until he explained in his quiet, serious way that he had never presented this copy to Searle because he'd been dissatisfied with the look of the finely handwritten salutation on the flyleaf. I was not so much surprised as stunned by what the simple explanation implied. After all, the entire *Juggler* is in Bob's very particular calligraphy, and I could only vaguely imagine how many times he'd done it over.

That thought brings me back again to 1952 on Eighth Street between Fifth and Sixth Avenues. The book was (and still is) bound in a dusky gray-blue paper over boards, and wonderfully, perfectly, the spine (and a bit more on either side) are in gold. I am frankly "fetishistic" about beautiful books and always have been. Some of my earliest, happiest experiences centered on the look, feel, and smell of books; reading was the least part of this sensual ritual. It was easy, then, for Blechman's binding to have promptly snared me; but what effectively sprung the trap was (and remember, I was seeing him for the very first time) Blechman's peculiar, sprawling calligraphy on the spine of his book. What did this modest, crooked, and seemingly "unprofessional" hand lettering have to do with the sophistication of dusty blue and gold? Everything. Cantalbert, our juggler, is, so to speak, already there on the spine and binding; the aesthetic essence of the work has quietly been stated. It is the perfect, brief overture to what is about to come. Such a gentle, abstract comment on the book's purpose is no easy business. But then, Blechman is no easy artist. As for my rhapsodizing over the exquisite variations in lettering on the title and copyright pages (there is a fierceness to the all-rights-reserved line compared to the trusting, open-eyed copyright line, and that juxtaposed with the charming certainty of his "a sort-of Christmas story"): if it sounds like too much precious conceit on my part—too bad! It's all there—suggesting so much—and we've not even begun the actual story! But I'll leave out the saga of the juggler—much has been written about him: he has won prestigious awards and been twice filmed. Besides, one purpose of the present volume—a work, in my opinion, long overdue—is to recreate this famous first book. If the reader is a genuine fetishist, then it will be his or her happy fate to seek out a first edition (it won't be easy to find—just great fun).

What multiple messages did the good *Juggler* pass on to this eager young artist? One could neatly list some of the more obvious: It offered hope that one day I might have autonomous control of a published work: that every detail, so crucial to the whole, could be rendered by the artist. It also encourage the latent wish to write one's own book and thus create—through story, pictures, type, layout, binding, choice of paper (and weight of paper), and overall design—a firm, personal statement. It suggested that elements, so intriguing and once considered contradictory, could be, with ingenuity, combined.

The comic strip, animated cartoon, and silent-movie comedy are all lovingly part of Blechman's background and style. For me, they were my nursery school of art. Mickey Mouse, Little Nemo, Krazy Kat, Charlie Chaplin, and Buster Keaton were the original sources, the wellsprings of excitement and creative stimulation. But these were, for me then, isolated forms navigating through my imagination like so many circling moons. *The Juggler,* in one giant step, pulled them together. The mix is so subtle, so understated, it might easily be overlooked. I was too eager and sniffing to miss the point. Here was a book that, with a magician's cool grace, brought it all off. The sheer surface look of it intrigued me. I was not to know then—or even imagine—how Blechman would wring every graphic ounce out of his wriggly style. It is, at first glance, a dangerous style for an artist to lock into. It's so specific, so special; where can you go from there? Blechman's refinement of that style—the paradox of his further condensing his miniature hieroglyphs to draw larger meanings—is a marvel.

It all has to do the man, of course. Blechman never took himself or his work too seriously. His *"mensch*-ness" expanded as he aged and the searching, stuttering line grew with him, though it seemed on paper to have nearly blown away. It became essence—the merest tool. His many imitators—the mass of counterfeit Blechmans who do indeed prove the folly of the entrapping style—are prisoners of style, helplessly bound to repeat themselves ad nauseam. Style, however, became Blechman's handmaiden, and rather than freezing into a permanent jitter, the Blechman look has a gorgeous fluidity. Every nuance and comic (or tragic) suggestion seems barely breathed on a page. His qualities of taste, intelligence, and—most vital—his instinct never to stray into forms that will betray him have allowed Blechman to express himself in a variety of ways that have enhanced the quality of American life. He has made his points in pages of *The New York Times Book Review,* on the covers of *The New Yorker,* and in too many other places to point out personal favorites.

I have very consciously stayed away from any analysis of Blechman's work—any groping with those much-mentioned themes, or coming out with a coherent "this is what Blechman is saying." That would be ludicrous, surely. Nor do I like putting his work (as some have) in large, suitable categories such as Fragile Man Against Unfeeling World. But there is one aspect of Blechman's art that touches me personally and is something of an obsession; I would even suggest it the unconscious bond that ties us together as artists. It is something I fleetingly mentioned earlier on: Blechman's child view. *Child view* is often translated into *creative view,* but they are not the same thing. There is a fierce, first freshness implied in the former that is part of an elaborate sensibility in the latter. This matter seriously concerns me because, as an artist doing books for children, I depend almost entirely on an uninhibited intercourse with this primitive, uncensored self.

A beautiful passage by Roger Shattuck, writing about the composer Erik Satie, comes to mind:

"The more one learns about Satie, the more one comes to see him as a man who performed every contortion in order to keep sight of his childhood. Like a child who twists his body as he walks in order not to lose sight of his shadow, Satie made sure that the most treasured part of his past was always at his side."

I personally can attest to the ordeal of maintaining the child vision in adult life, and I suspect Blechman has suffered the same dual perception. But it is this very quality that informs his work and accounts for its unique appeal.

MAURICE SENDAK
Ridgefield, Connecticut
February 17, 1980

(an excerpt from the Foreword to
R. O. Blechman: Behind the Lines, published in 1980)

A
sort-of
CHRISTMAS
STORY

CANTALBERT WAS A Juggler.

Every morning he would walk to
town with his Equipment, ...

TOWN gate

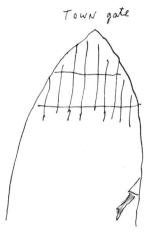

. . . Unpack his DISCS, balancing CHAIR,
HOOPS and BALLS, . . .

... and JUGGLE.

But he could Never ATTRACT AN AUDIENCE.

He tried NEW and DIFFICULT tricks.

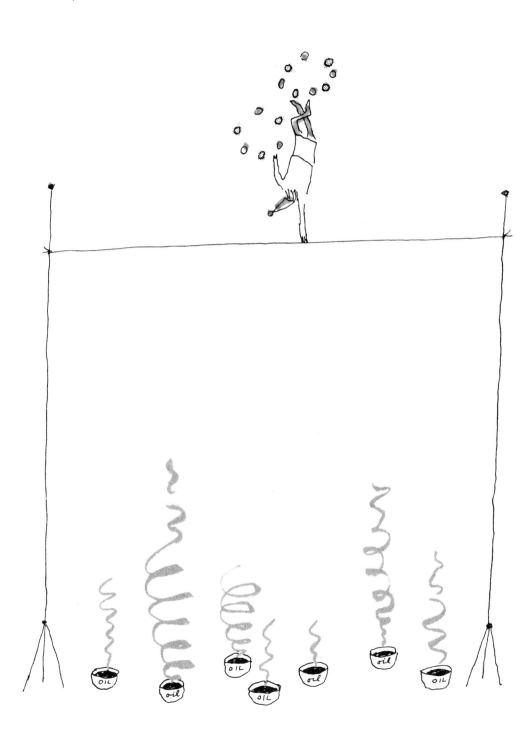

BUT nobody PAID ANY ATTENTION TO HIM.

CANTALBERT was UNHAPPY. He wanted his juggling to REFORM THE WORLD.

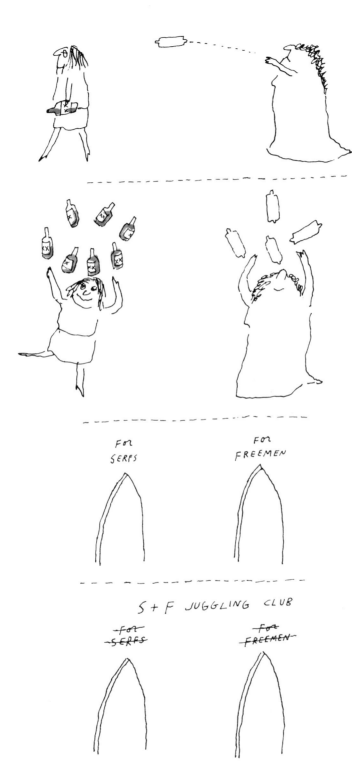

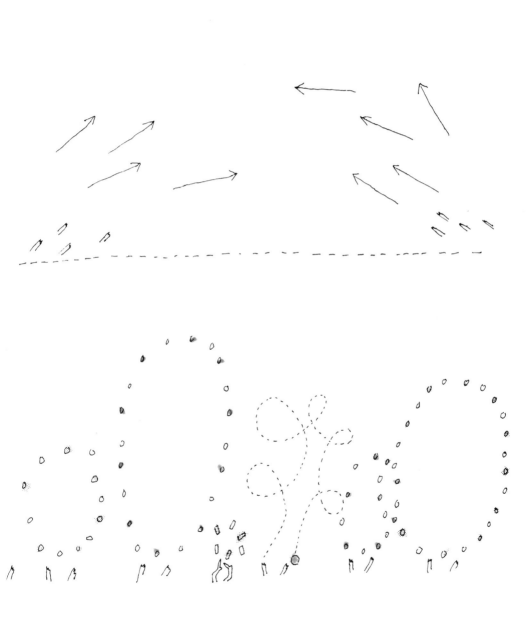

But Nobody WOULD PAY ATTENTION TO HIM.

poof

Then CANTALBERT decided that if he were more ASCETIC, Heaven would give him audiences. THE NEXT DAY he stood on his RIGHT HAND for TWO HOURS.

And the blood
flowed down
from his
feet.

BUT HE STILL DID NOT ATTRACT an audience.

THEN CANTALBERT THOUGHT:
Perhaps I was not ascetic enough.
So he ran to the market...

... and bought CARROTS,...

... and SUGAR beets,...

...and SCISSORS,...

... and STRING,...

... and ...

snip
snip
snip

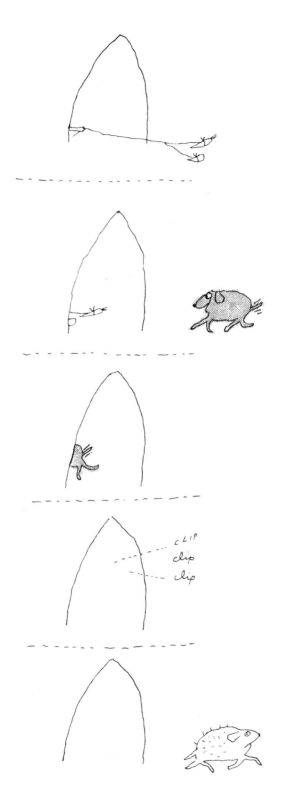

CLIP
clip
clip

...and CANTALBERT made himself a HAIRCOAT.

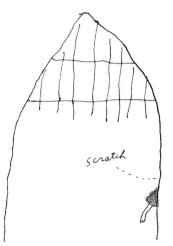

But ONLY A FEW ASCETICS watched him.

CANTALBERT was a FAILURE

He realized the world would never change
and in fifty years he would be DEAD...

... and turn into dust...

... and blow across fields...

... and nourish cowslips...

... and blow into people's eyes...

DAMN!

... AND HIS PINK and COCOA HOOPS, and DISCS, and BALLS WOULD MEAN nothing, NOTHING AT ALL.

IF ONLY HE WERE A MONK he could live in a warm room...

... and have friends, ...

... and feed the birds ...

..and he would be far away from UNHAPPINESS.

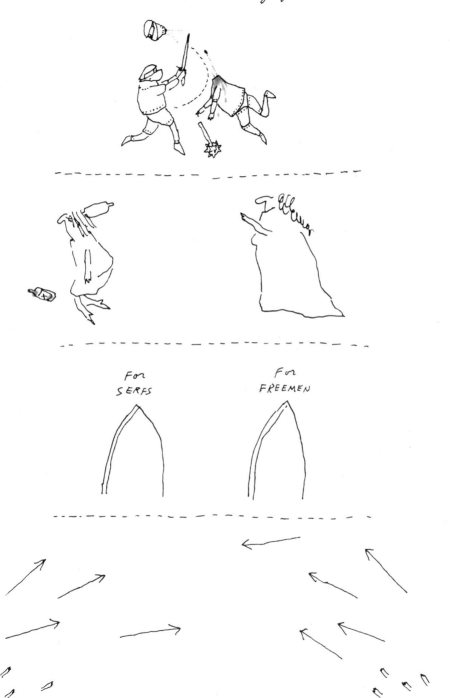

For
SERFS

For
FREEMEN

... and he would tell MARY of how sad and lonely he was ...

... and She would Understand.

MONASTERY

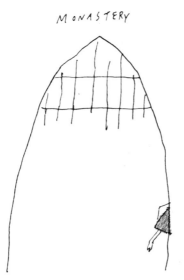

Cantalbert was accepted and he immediately
changed into a FRESH ROBE and...

... ATE HIS FIRST MEAL in the monastery.
ALL THE BROTHERS SAID Latin PRAYERS.

THE meal concluded with the singing of
AGNUS DEI.

Then CANTALBERT visited the brothers in their CUBicles.

One Brother copied manuscripts

Another Painted Frescoes

Others taught children the GOSPEL...

LAZARUS

JESUS RAISED HIM FROM THE DEAD

DUNCE

... and wrote poems to the VIRGIN.

CONTRESTARI!
CONTEMPLAR!

... and CARVED MADONNAS ...

... and COOKED ...

... and composed MUSIC.

But CANTALBERT could neither PAINT, COPY, TEACH, SCULPT, WRITE, COOK, or COMPOSE.

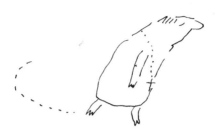

He could not even say an AVE MARIA or SING AN Agnus Dei.

He was USELESS.

HE COULD DO nothing.

THE next morning he decided to ASSIST THE COOK.
HE WAS TOLD TO KILL A GOOSE FOR DINNER.

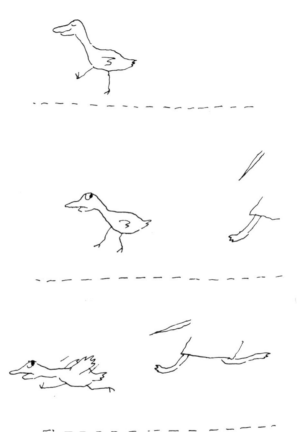

HONK
honk
honk

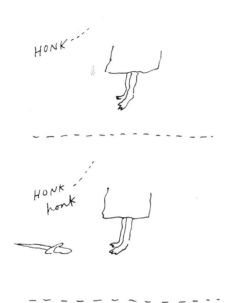

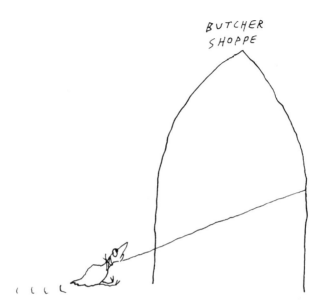

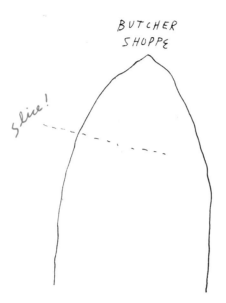

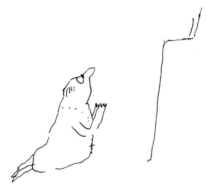

Then Cantalbert was told HOW TO
prepare the GOOSE...

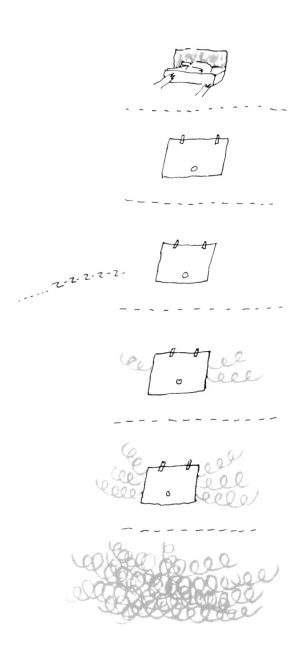

KITCHEN

KITCHEN

Then Cantalbert tried to COPY MANUSCRIPTS.

He TRIED TO PAINT FRESCOES.

HE TRIED TO TEACH THE GOSPEL.

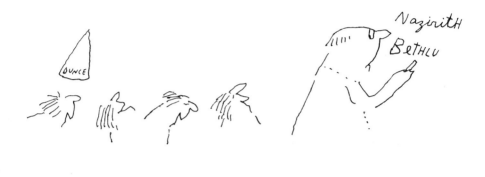

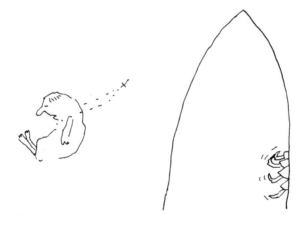

POETRY
ROOM

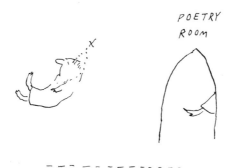

SCULPTURE
ROOM

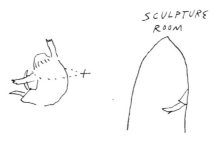

TREATISE
ROOM

MUSIC
ROOM

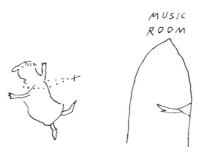

The Brothers COMPLAINED of CANTALBERT to the
ABBOT,...

... but the ABBOT permitted him to remain among them if he would do ODD-JOBS FOR THE MONASTERY.

Chimney

He shovelled the snow

carried the groceries

swept the floors

and washed the windows

SOON IT BEGAN TO SNOW heavily...

. . . and CHristmas grew near.

All the brothers retired to their cubicles...

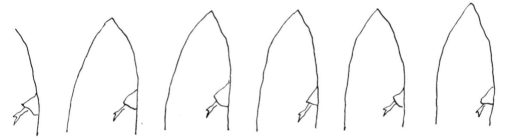

... and prepared their Christmas presents to Honor the Virgin.

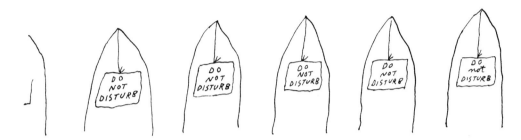

THE WRITERS WROTE

scratch
scratch

Stone Carvers CARVED

chip
chip

THE COOK COOKED

THE POET POETICIZED

SOUL
aha!
EXTOLL

The Composer COMPOSED

The PAINTER PAINTED

Swoosh
SWOOSH

BUT CANTALBERT DID NOT KNOW what to do

?

?

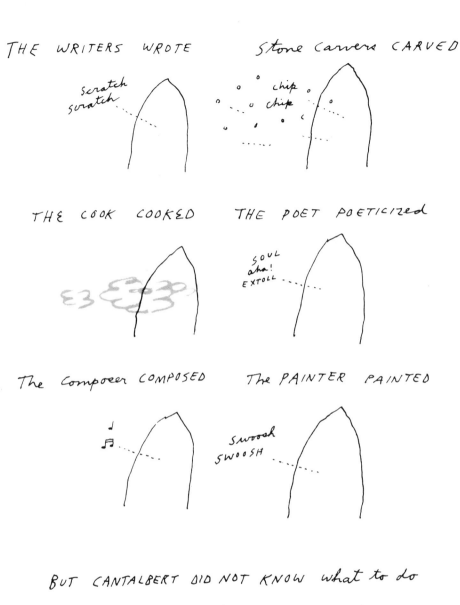

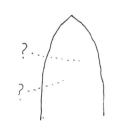

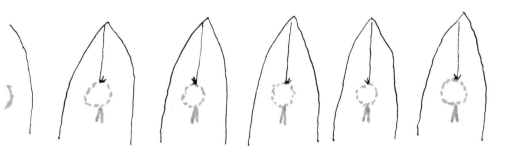

Everybody went to the chapel to present
Gifts to the VIRGIN

BUT CANTALBERT WENT last BECAUSE HE
HAD nothing TO GIVE MARY.

THE COOK was the first to present his Gift:
He gave Mary a Cake,
THE CHURCH TRIUMPHANT.

Brother MAURICE read MARY a latin poem
he had composed.

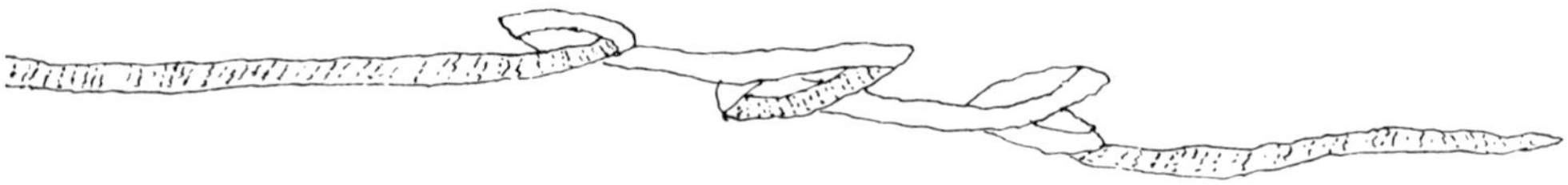

Brother Armand presented the Virgin with
THE SMALLEST ILLUMINATED BIBLE EVER MADE.

Brother Fulbert dedicated his Choral Work to the VIRGIN.

Brother GUILLAME gave Mary a Triptych
of THE VIRGIN AND THE DONOR,...

... and Brother THOMAS presented his ivory carving, THE CHRIST CHILD.

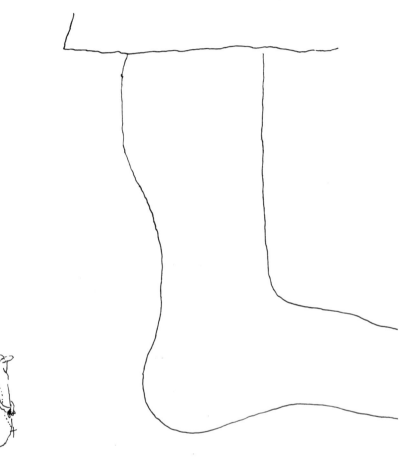

But CANTALBERT HAD NOTHING HE COULD GIVE.

That night, ...

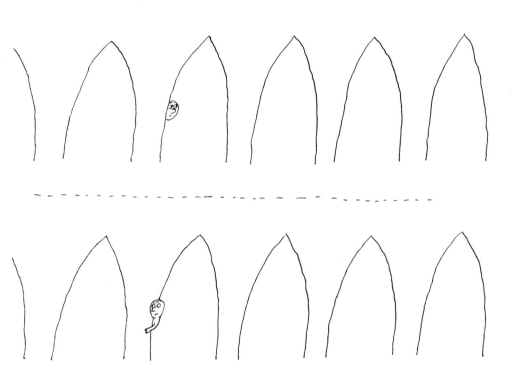

... CANTALBERT tip-toed INTO THE CHAPEL.

Tip   Toe   Tip   Toe   Tip

Tip   Toe   Tip   TOE   tip   toe   Tip   toe   Tip   TOE

CHAPEL

tip   toe   tip   toe   TIP   toe   TIP   toe   tip   t

HE JUGGLED ALL NIGHT to ENTERTAIN MARY.

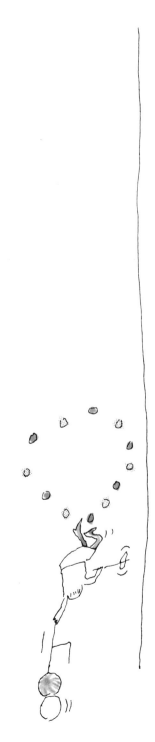

And the blood
flowed down
From his
feet.

When morning came, The Brothers ran
to the chapel to admire their gifts again.

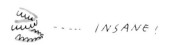 ----- INSANE!

----- Sacrilege!

----- MONSTROUS!

--- Desecration!

---- MAD!

...en Cantalbert collapsed from Exhaustion.

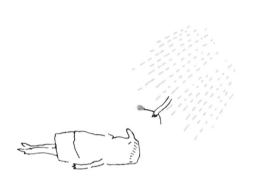

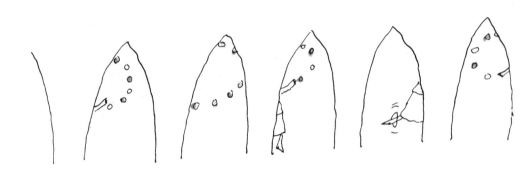